presented to

by

date

I HAVE SEEN A BEAUTIFUL LEGACY OF HOPE *through faith handed down from one generation* **to the next.**

~ DONNA SCHULLER

A LEGACY of Success

DONNA SCHULLER

WITH STORIES FROM THE FAMILY

Robert SCHULLER I ❧ *Robert* SCHULLER II ❧ *Robert* SCHULLER III

J. Countryman
Nashville, Tennessee

Project editor: Jenny Baumgartner

Designed by Koechel Peterson and Associates, Inc., Minneapolis, Minnesota

ISBN 0-8499-5709-5

Printed and bound in the United States of America

www.jcountryman.com

PREFACE

For nearly seventeen years, I have observed and been a part of an incredible family experience. Through the family leadership of my father-in-law, Robert Schuller I, and alongside my husband and best friend, Robert II, I have grown closer to God and have gained a deeper understanding of myself than I ever thought I could. As I've also helped to raise Robert III, who is now a remarkable young man of nineteen, I have seen a beautiful legacy of hope through faith handed down from one generation to the next. I have witnessed the power of overcoming challenges through perseverance, confident in the knowledge that God will work things out for good. I have seen what it means to live with integrity and commitment in making the choices that are right, though not always easy. I have seen worthwhile goals come to fruition by keeping your eyes focused on God and what He has in store for your life.

In my family, I have seen these things flourish through positive words of encouragement, consistency in values, time spent with one another, good humor, and lots of love and physical affection. The foundation and role model of our legacy is Jesus Christ, a perfect God who loves, guides, and protects.

What is a legacy of success? How do we know if we are

succeeding in passing on a legacy that will encourage hope for tomorrow? The dictionary defines legacy as "a gift by will," but I believe that a legacy is not always willfully passed on. Some of our family's habits and rituals seem to be "absorbed," sometimes without intent. The purpose of this book is to illustrate these habits and the positive effect they have on our children and will have on our children's children for ages to come.

I recently complimented my husband and thanked him for driving the children to school each morning. As in most families with children in the home, mornings are not always peaceful. Getting in a car with two, sometimes bickering, children is not always a pleasant experience. But Robert has decided to make this his responsibility, even when he has early morning appointments himself. This drive in the car is his time alone with the kids. Most importantly, he has a wonderful habit of praying with them just before they leave the car. He does this even when they are frustrated and late!

While gathering the stories for this book, he and I talked about this morning ritual, and he told me that his father had done the same thing with him and his sisters, something I never knew. This seemingly "little thing" has been passed down to the next generation. I believe with all my heart that even though children won't always do what you say, they will most likely do what you do. The habits that we form today will become part of our family's legacy tomorrow.

In sharing some of the Schuller-family legacy in this book, my hope is that you will see a glimpse of some of the spirit that makes our family prosper in love. In the pages that follow, you will read stories from me and from three generations of Robert Schullers: Robert I, my father-in-law; Robert II, my husband; and Robert III, my stepson. My prayer is that as you read these stories, you will see how you, too, can pass on a legacy of success. You will see that there truly is hope for tomorrow! ✍

⌒ DONNA SCHULLER
Summer 2000

$\mathcal{W}$e rejoice in the hope of the glory of God.

Not only so, but we also rejoice in our sufferings, because we know that

suffering produces perseverance; perseverance, character; and character, hope.

Section I

Seedling... Trust

THE POSSIBILITIES OF FAITH

HOW DO POSITIVE-THINKING PEOPLE SAY "YES" WITHOUT BEING BLINDED BY POTENTIAL FAILURE, OBSTACLES, AND DIFFICULTIES?

Dare to say "yes"! I have tried to live this. I want it to be my witness. I'm seventy-three years old, and from childhood, I've been a "yes" man, never a "no" person. And I call you to be a "yes" person—but with conditions attached.

"Yes, if this is right and if it is God's will."

"Yes, if God is guiding you, motivating you, and if He is entrusting you with His idea."

"Yes, if" starts with a big *if.*

"Yes, when . . . God puts a desire and a passion within you that you can't dismiss."

"Yes, when . . . doors open that you can't explain."

"Yes, after . . . you are really committed to doing God's work and God's will."

"Yes, after . . . you have checked the price." What is it going to cost? Jesus made it clear: Everything that is nice has its price.

My kids have grown up with the "yes, if"; "yes, when"; and "yes, after." I have said, "Yes, after you are married" and "Yes, when . . . if . . . and after you know the price."

You know the price you'll have to pay to succeed, but you also know what price you are going to have to pay if you walk away and ignore what's in your hand.

What's in your hand? What visions can you see for your life tomorrow? How can you make a difference in the world?

We need young people who will say, "Lord, yes, I'll be a leader for You." We need them in the ministry. I'm asking you, does God want you to be a minister like I am? Will you some-day wear the robe?

For people who are in the middle of life, what will you say if God has another career planned for you? Will you dare to say "yes"?

The book of Joshua ends with a dramatic conclusion. Joshua is about to lead three thousand Israelites into the Promised Land where they'll encounter giants, and it is a place where the religion of Baal is celebrated. Does he dare lead them into this country? Will God's people continue to serve the one true Lord? Joshua decides that he must first challenge them by saying, ". . . choose for yourselves this day whom you will serve." Joshua decides, "But as for me and my house, we will serve the Lord" (Josh. 24:15).

Possibility thinkers are people of faith who say, "Yes. Yes. Yes." Dare to say "yes" to God. He is calling you. I don't know what lies before you. It may be risky. Trust Him, stay connect-ed with Him, and He will bless you. 🖋

~ ROBERT SCHULLER I

BE STRONG AND OF GOOD COURAGE; DO NOT BE AFRAID, NOR BE DISMAYED, FOR THE LORD YOUR GOD IS WITH YOU WHEREVER YOU GO.

JOSHUA 1:9

DARE TO SAY
"*yes*"
TO GOD.

~ ROBERT SCHULLER I

Into the Light

Recently, I was in Hawaii with my family
and friends, and we visited one of the most
beautiful bays in the entire world, Hanauma Bay.

We put on our snorkels and fins and paddled around to look at all of the beautiful sea life beneath the surface of the ocean. We also hiked just around the point of Hanauma Bay to a place called the "toilet bowl," which is named for the currents that come into this opening in the rocks. When the current enters, the opening swells and fills with water. When the water goes out, the "bowl" completely empties of water, much like a flushing toilet. We jumped into this hole and were lifted up and down by the water over and over. What fun we had!

Then I discovered something new. Not far from the "toilet bowl" is a small hole in the rock where the ocean shoots out and then flows back down. One swell after another, the water shoots up out of this "keyhole" and then disappears.

As we were standing at the "keyhole," a man came and lay down next to it. When the next swell came, he dove into the hole headfirst and disappeared. Fifteen to twenty seconds later, he re-appeared in the channel about fifteen feet away. *Wow! That's scary*, I thought. Then I said, "I've got to do that!" My wife said, "No, you're not." But I love exciting challenges, and I said, "He did it. It looks like fun. I'm going to do it, too!"

When the water came up, I dove in headfirst. To my surprise, I found myself in pure darkness. I was in a cave. Off in the distance, through the murky water, I could see a small hole of light, so I knew where I needed to go. I swam the breaststroke as hard as I could toward this light, but I got nowhere. My heart started to race as I paddled harder. Still, I couldn't move. Then, suddenly the swell moved in another direction and pulled me right into the channel, into the light. There, I came to the surface to take my first breath.

That experience reminds me of our faith. If you find yourself in difficult circumstances, or in a situation that is surrounded with darkness, and you feel like you may not be able to get your breath, then put your faith in God. Believe! Trust! And realize that God will carry you into the light! ✄

~ ROBERT SCHULLER II

> But you are a chosen generation...His own special people, that you may proclaim the praises of Him who called you out of darkness into His marvelous light.
>
> **1 PETER 2:9**

Dad's Patience

If you know my family, then you know that we are avid fishermen. We love fish—big fish, small fish, blue fish, striped fish, fish with tails, fish with big teeth. But there is no fish like the marlin, and I will never forget when I caught my first one.

I was twelve years old, and my father was trying to convince me that I could catch one of these monsters. Though it had been a long-standing dream of mine, I never quite believed that a ninety-pound kid like me could pull in a two-hundred-pound fish like that. In fact, I'm not sure anyone thought it was possible—except my dad. "It's not about strength; it's about finesse," he would say.

We were coming in from a long and tiring trip—empty-handed. I could see the shore just a few miles from the boat as we were slowly dragging the marlin jigs behind us. Desperately wanting to return to the shore, I said, "Let's reel 'em in, Dad." But Dad kept saying, "Just a little longer, just a little longer." Finally, we bargained that in five minutes, we would quit and head for home.

I was impatiently counting the seconds when I heard it:

"ppzzzzzzz," the sound of the line being pulled out by . . . something. My heart jumped. "Fish on! Fish on!" I cried as I jumped down and set the hook. To my amazement, a beautiful marlin leapt out of the clear blue water. After a struggle, I did it: I pulled in my first marlin.

Even though I lacked the faith in myself to accomplish the task, my father believed in me. He knew I could catch a marlin. He cheered me on as I was reeling it in, and it was only because of his patience in me that I succeeded. He mirrored God's patience and faith.

God believes in you. Your Father, your Savior, and your Friend—He will be with you, holding your hand until the end. No matter what you're going through, be patient. I promise that you will experience victory. 🌿

~ ROBERT SCHULLER III

But the ones that fell on the good ground are those who, having heard the word with a noble and good heart, keep it and bear fruit with patience.
LUKE 8:15

EVEN THOUGH I LACKED
THE FAITH IN MYSELF TO
ACCOMPLISH THE TASK,
my father believed in me.
~ ROBERT SCHULLER III

AN UNLIKELY MEETING

THE MOST COMMON QUESTION THAT I AM ASKED IS
"HOW DID YOU MEET YOUR HUSBAND?" A LITTLE SMILE
ALWAYS APPEARS ON MY FACE WHEN I RECALL OUR UNLIKELY
MEETING ALMOST SEVENTEEN YEARS AGO. IT WAS AT A
TIME IN MY LIFE WHEN THINGS WEREN'T GOING AS
I HAD HOPED THEY WOULD BE.

I had been working for an airline for seven years, but the
company had to declare bankruptcy. Obviously, I was out of a
job. At about the same time, my husband of only a few years
decided he didn't want to be married any longer. Unsure of
what to do, I moved back to my hometown of Laguna Beach,
California. I thought that all of my hopes and dreams had
been stripped from me, and I was feeling angry and discon-
nected from God. I realize now, of course, that God was
preparing me for what was to come.

I first saw him in the parking garage of my apartment
complex. He was carrying a very large briefcase, and since
there were very few young people living in my building, I
assumed that he was a door-to-door salesman of some kind.
I would learn several months later that he was indeed a kind
of a "salesman." He sold hope, faith, and God's love—three
things that I certainly needed at that lowest point in my life.

Months went by. On December 26, 1983, I was looking
out of my apartment window and saw him again on the

balcony below. I remember thinking, "He can't be selling door-to-door the day after Christmas; he must live here." I ran to my room to freshen up and decided that I would go and introduce myself. By the time I had finished, however, he was gone. I decided to go to plan B: I took the stairs to the beach and walked down to shoreline. It was a cold and misty day, and I was bundled up in a warm-up suit, socks, and tennis shoes.

THEREFORE, IF ANYONE IS IN CHRIST, HE IS A NEW CREATION; OLD THINGS HAVE PASSED AWAY; BEHOLD, ALL THINGS HAVE BECOME NEW.
2 CORINTHIANS 5:17

I wasn't down at the beach for more than ten minutes before I looked up and saw him walking toward me. I knew that he was coming to speak to me since there was no one else on the beach; it was too cold! I still remember what he was wearing: blue jeans, a red plaid shirt, a beige windbreaker, and brown cowboy boots. We said "hello" and began to converse. He said that his name was Robert Schuller and that he was a minister. I didn't recognize his name, but later, my roommate told me about the Crystal Cathedral. Surprisingly, she and her family watched the "Hour of Power" on television on Sunday mornings.

As Robert and I continued our conversations, he told me that his wife had asked for a divorce, and he shared all about his two little children, then ages two and five. I remember thinking, *Oh boy, I thought I had a difficult situation; I certainly don't need this!* And when he told me that he was a minister, it intimidated me. I hadn't been to church in several years. I remember feeling a combination of curiosity and guilt—but this would prove to be no accidental meeting.

We quickly developed a deep friendship and respect. I know that we helped each other through some very difficult times. We soon fell in love, and nearly a year later, in November of 1984, we were married.

Sometimes God takes the most unlikely circumstances and molds them into things of beauty and productivity. He takes the brokenness in our lives, and through His love, He forgives, He heals, He inspires, and . . . He continues to re-create us, if we trust Him. ✄

~ DONNA SCHULLER

SOMETIMES GOD TAKES THE MOST UNLIKELY CIRCUMSTANCES
AND MOLDS THEM INTO THINGS OF BEAUTY AND PRODUCTIVITY.
~ DONNA SCHULLER

PASS IT ON

MY WIFE AND I BOTH COME FROM THE DUTCH TRADITION. MY PARENTS AND GRANDPARENTS ON BOTH SIDES, AS WELL AS MY WIFE'S FAMILY, HAVE ALL COME FROM THE NETHERLANDS. THEY WERE IMMIGRANTS TO AMERICA, AND THEY LIVED IN A DUTCH COMMUNITY IN IOWA.

It was our families' custom to pray a blessing before meals and a prayer of thanksgiving after meals. We never left the table without saying "thank you." After the noon meal, we not only said the usual prayers, but my father also would

LORD,
YOU HAVE BEEN
OUR DWELLING
PLACE IN ALL
GENERATIONS.
PSALM 90:1

reach under the table to a special shelf where he kept the family Bible. He would take out the Bible and read a chapter. That's the kind of family I come from: we read one Bible chapter every day.

The Psalms were the preferred Bible readings in my family. In my parents' days, the Dutch people in the Netherlands did not sing the hymns of Luther or Wesley when they went to church; instead, they sang the Psalms of David and Moses. The Psalms were put to melody, and the "psalm singers" would sing with profound gusto.

Unlike many surrounding countries, the Protestant Christians in the Netherlands felt profound affection and respect for the Jewish people because they were the people of the Psalms; they were the people of Moses and the prophets. That's why the Netherlands became the number one place for the Underground Railroad, which saved many Jewish people from the Holocaust. The windmills served as the stations to hide the Jews who were escaping from the Nazis. If the coast was clear, the windmill would form a cross. If the area was under surveillance by the Gestapo, the windmill would form an *X*, meaning, "Don't stop here; we are being watched."

Psalm 90 was a favorite chapter in our family when I was growing up. It begins, "Lord, through all the generations you have been our home" (90:1, NLT). After the reading, my father would give his little sermon: "What is a home? What is a dwelling place? It is a place where there is security and where one feels safe. It is a place where you feel love and acceptance. It is a place where you feel honored."

~ ROBERT SCHULLER I

AFTER THE READING, MY FATHER WOULD GIVE HIS LITTLE SERMON: "WHAT IS A HOME? WHAT IS A DWELLING PLACE? IT IS A PLACE WHERE THERE IS SECURITY AND WHERE ONE FEELS SAFE."

~ROBERT SCHULLER I

Stand in the Gap

As a student at Oral Roberts University, I am required to attend chapel every Wednesday and Friday. These services have a way of being boring at times, but one day, we heard a speaker named Eastman Curtis who was anything but dull. When he said, "Open your Bibles to . . ." twenty or so students jumped up, yelled, and waved their Bibles in the air. They were members of Eastman's church.

Pastor Curtis said, "Hallelujah! Those guys are excited because we are about to read the Word!" He then encouraged all five thousand of us to do the same thing. With my fellow students, I jumped up, waved my Bible in the air, and yelled with excitement. Our university president, Richard Roberts, didn't attend the service that morning, so Pastor Curtis convinced us to yell the same shouts of praise on Friday. I could just see it: President Roberts saying, "Open your Bibles to . . ." and the whole place going up in a roar.

When Friday morning came, everyone was talking about the "big gag" that was about to occur. Sure enough, President Roberts stepped up to the podium and, as always,

So I sought for a man among them who would make a wall, and stand in the gap before Me on behalf of the land, that I should not destroy it; but I found no one.

EZEKIEL 22:30

said, "Open your Bibles to . . ." The whole student body twitched, but no one stood. Everyone was waiting for someone else to stand first. An eerie silence fell over the building for about three seconds. But then, a friend of mine, Deidre, jumped up, held her Bible in the air, and screamed at the top of her lungs. In an instant, the whole place went up with a great cry.

It's amazing that all five thousand of us knew exactly what to do, but none of us did it because we didn't have the guts. It took one person, just one, to do the right thing, and then everyone else followed.

God has called you to do something great. It may seem a little scary, but He needs believers who will be leaders for Him, who will stand strong in the gap.

~ ROBERT SCHULLER III

GOD HAS CALLED YOU TO DO SOMETHING GREAT.
It may seem a little scary, but He needs believers
who will be leaders for Him, who will stand
strong in the gap.
~ ROBERT SCHULLER III

Too Good Not to Be True

At our local theater, large employee groups can purchase tickets at a special rate. Instead of paying $7 for a movie, groups pay only $4.50. I once bought a dozen group tickets, thinking I'd surely use them all before the end of the year.

One day, I noticed that the tickets were nearing their expiration date, and I still had ten of them left. So I decided to take the family to a movie, and I brought all of my extra tickets with me.

When we arrived, there was a long line for tickets. I thought to myself, "This will be shoe in. I'll just go down the line, and I'll sell these people a ticket for only $4. I'll take a $.50 hit, but the person buying the ticket will save $3." So I approached the first people in line and said, "Hey, I've got group activity tickets. Would you like to buy any?" They looked at me like I was nuts. Maybe it was the fact that I had my hat on, hadn't shaved that day, and was wearing my Levi's and a sweatshirt. I looked rather grubby. Perhaps if I had been wearing my suit and tie, then I would have had better luck.

As I went down the line, I tried to explain what a good deal the tickets were, but I couldn't sell even one. I was amazed! *Why would anyone pay full price when they could buy a ticket from me for $3 less?* I thought. But no one would do it—that is, until one person finally had enough courage to say, "So . . . so what is that?" I explained, "They're group activity tickets. Look at them. They are even printed on cloth paper. It's obvious that they're not counterfeits. Go on. I'm waiting in line right behind you. If you have a problem, I'll return your money." He agreed to buy one. Then somebody else said, "Okay, I'll buy one." And all of a sudden, like magic, they all sold.

I couldn't believe how difficult it was to break through the skepticism of the masses of people who wouldn't trust and believe me. Here I was, with this wonderful opportunity for them—the same ticket at almost half the price—but they wouldn't take advantage of it. And yet, I believe that the message of Jesus Christ is received in much the same way today. It sounds almost too good to be true. And we've been raised with such skeptical minds that we say, "Is the grace of Jesus Christ real? Surely, there's a catch." We come up with all kinds of reasons not to believe.

The bottom line is that Jesus Christ comes to each of us, and He offers a gift—the gift of everlasting life. Whoever believes in Him will not perish but have everlasting life. When we understand that we can surrender everything to Jesus and can trust Him, then we can succeed. 🦋

~ ROBERT SCHULLER II

FOLLOWING THE CALL OF GOD

THE POWER OF THE SPOKEN WORD IS INCREDIBLY STRONG. WORDS CAN LIFT A PERSON UP THROUGH ENCOURAGEMENT, OR THEY CAN PUSH A PERSON DOWN WITH CRITICISM AND JUDGEMENT.

Recently, I was reminded of this while talking with a friend of mine. She is a teacher at the Christian school at Rancho Capistrano, a 175-acre ranch that is a part of the Crystal Cathedral Ministries. My friend and I were discussing how important it is to speak positive words to children because children often rise to the level you expect of them.

Unfortunately, many children hear negative messages; nonetheless, through the miracle of God's intervention, they can mature into successful individuals. With God's help, these children can rise above earthly expectations and answer the heavenly call.

My friend shared with me an example of one such child. She told me the touching story about her father, Dr. David Spindle, whom I have known and admired for years. He and his wife, Polly, are former members of our church. In recent years, they retired and moved to Alaska.

When David was in the fourth grade, he was given an IQ test. He recalls, "The second question on the test involved getting a mouse through a maze. You had to draw a line from the mouse to the cheese at the center. I immediately picked up my pencil and started at the center. I worked my way out toward the mouse, but I suddenly realized that this might be cheating because the question clearly stated, 'Take the mouse to the cheese.' I then erased all of my lines and started again. By this time, the maze had become a horrible blotch of pencil erasing. The bell rang, and I hadn't even finished the second question to the test."

Not surprisingly, the results of the test confused the teacher, who concluded that David "didn't have an IQ." When David asked his mother what this meant, she laughed and said that his teacher "didn't think he was very smart."

Years later in his college psychology class, David was given another IQ test. This time, he scored above two hundred. Because his score was uncommonly high, he and his professor simply laughed; neither thought David could possess such remarkable intelligence. A few years later in medical school, however, David was given yet another IQ test. The battery of tests lasted two days. When the results came back, the professor remarked, "These are the highest scores I've ever seen. This makes me think that you are really in need of counseling."

His professor also said, "With your intelligence, you have no need of religion. It is only for the weak." David's professor believed that a person with a genius IQ had no

Let us run with endurance the race that is set before us.
HEBREWS 12:1

need for Christianity or any other "archaic" religious beliefs. He recommended that David withdraw from medical school. David became very concerned and met with the head of the psychiatry department. In response, the department director laughed and said, "Don't worry. Just get back to work. It will all turn out all right."

Because of his perseverance, determination, and skill, David became one of the nation's first neurosurgeons with nearly forty years in practice and thirty-five years as an adjunct faculty member in the department of neurosurgery at Loma Linda University. David says, "I do not believe that I have no IQ or that I am a genius. Rather, I am somewhere in between. I would urge people not to put too much faith in a test. Instead, put your faith in God and His power to work through you, and you will succeed."

Well-meaning people will often say things that can injure our spirits and cause us to believe that we are less than God made us to be. If you follow the call of God, He will encourage you and help show you the way to success. ✍

~ DONNA SCHULLER

Section
II

Sapling... Faith

Recharge Your Spiritual Battery Daily

We all have gadgets in our homes with rechargeable batteries. My portable telephone has a rechargeable battery, and when I leave it off the base too long, it goes dead. I also have a battery in my car. Recently, when I came back from vacation, I tried to start my car, but nothing happened. The battery was dead. I had to charge it up again before I could drive it.

Our lives are like batteries. We need to recharge our spiritual batteries daily. After all, we are not energizer bunnies. We can't keep "going and going and going."

Wally Amos, originator of Famous Amos Cookies, once said to me, "Robert, every day, I used to call my mother on the phone, and I'd read the Good Book, the Bible, to her."

I asked, "Every day?"

He responded, "Yeah, every day, I'd call her up, and I'd read the Good Book to her, and I'd ask her to give me an 'amen,' and she'd say, 'AMEN!' I did that until the day she died. You see, she couldn't read, but she needed to hear God's Word. So I would call her on the telephone, and I would read it to her."

During my childhood, our family always read the Bible at mealtime. My parents' families did it, and my grandparents' families did it, and my great-grandparents' families probably did it. When I visit my aunts and uncles, they have that same spiritual habit. After dinner, they take out the Bible and read a chapter. Then, the bookmark goes in, and the next day, they read another chapter. I have raised my children on dinnertime Bible devotions as well.

Did you know that if you spend fifteen minutes a day reading the Bible, you will be able to read the entire Bible from cover to cover in one year? Start this habit in your family today. It's fantastic. ✍

~ ROBERT SCHULLER II

He who has begun a good work in you will complete it until the day of Christ.

PHILIPPIANS 1:6

Our lives are like batteries.
WE NEED TO RECHARGE OUR SPIRITUAL BATTERIES DAIL
~ ROBERT SCHULLER II

The Good News

I will never forget the first time I led someone to Jesus. I was a new Christian and had received Christ only a few months earlier, so I was nervous and excited at the same time.

A friend from school was having a birthday party and invited me to come. Unfortunately, it wasn't the party I had expected. When the first person I met asked me to smoke marijuana with him, I knew there weren't very many Christians there. My first instinct would have been to turn around and go back home, but I knew in my heart that I needed to stay for some reason.

"I'm gonna win someone to Christ," I said under my breath. Later in the evening, I found myself talking to a girl named Christi. Christi was heavy into drugs and recently had been introduced to the occult by her boyfriend, who was a devoted member. I talked to her for almost two hours. At first, we were just talking about normal everyday things, but soon, the conversation changed. Christi began to cry and tell me all about what was going on in her life. I couldn't believe it, but I began to share with her about how much Jesus loves her and how she is not alone. It was the easiest thing I had ever done. That night, I prayed with Christi to receive salvation and healing. I was so excited!

Go therefore and make disciples of all the nations, baptizing them in the name of the Father, and of the Son and of the Holy Spirit, teaching them to observe all things that I have commanded you; and lo, I am with you always, even to the end of the age.

MATTHEW 28:19

I felt an indescribable joy within me that I had never felt before as I watched Jesus come into her life. Christi stopped taking drugs and is now helping lead the youth group at her local church.

That experience set off a desire in me to share the Gospel of Jesus Christ. I believe that every child of God is called to witness, whether to those in the workplace, at school, or on the mission field. God has called each of us to be a bright light in a dark world.

Tell someone the Good News. Tell someone today how much Jesus loves them, how He died to set them free from guilt and sin, and you will experience the same joy that I felt—a joy that comes from the Lord. ✄

~ ROBERT SCHULLER III

TELL someone today how much Jesus loves them,
how He died to set them free from guilt and sin,
and you will experience the same joy that I felt—
A JOY THAT COMES FROM THE LORD.

THE LORD OF YOUR CONSCIENCE

WITHOUT FREEDOM, WE ARE DEAD, BUT WHEN FREEDOM IS UNCONTROLLED AND UNREDEEMED, WE OPEN THE DOOR TO EVIL. SO HOW DO WE MONITOR FREEDOM? WE NEED OUR FREEDOM, BUT WHAT WE NEED FIRST IS A SAVIOR LIKE JESUS TO TAKE THE TAPROOT OF POTENTIAL EVIL OUT OF OUR SOULS FOREVER.

We need a Savior like Jesus, and then we need a Lord like Christ. Great theologians like John Calvin have said that the only freedom that can be retained and restrained is the freedom that places the Lordship of Jesus Christ over your conscience.

What is a conscience? It is really the proof of God and the moral law within. Conscience is something that has been lost in America during the last ten, twenty, and even thirty years. I don't know when and how it was lost.

There is a great lack of conscience when kids obtain guns and then shoot their classmates in school. I was in Littleton, Colorado, after the high school shootings, and I hugged and cried with many people. I haven't gotten over it, and I don't think I ever will. When I was growing up, the children I knew had a conscience.

IF YOU ABIDE IN MY WORD, YOU ARE MY DISCIPLES INDEED. AND YOU SHALL KNOW THE TRUTH AND THE TRUTH SHALL MAKE YOU FREE.

JOHN 8:32

Forty-four years ago, a twenty-eight-year-old young man was ringing doorbells in the new suburbs of Orange County, California. He had black hair, and his name was Robert Schuller. He asked "unchurched" people to come to church, and many of them came. I still remember those years.

As I walked from door to door, people would sometimes say to me, "Oh, Dr. Schuller, lots of good people live on our street. They are wonderful people, but they don't go to church and they don't send their kids to Sunday school." Then they would ask me, "Dr. Schuller, what is going to happen to those kids when they grow up and they don't know the Ten Commandments or the Beatitudes and nothing about religion at all? What's going to happen to them? What kind of a country will we have?"

We have that kind of country today, like it or not. A lot of good people—intelligent people, educated people, people in powerful positions—were never taught anything about the Bible or Jesus.

Forty years have passed. Now those people have children and grandchildren, and secularism has become so deep and wide in our culture that God is not part of it, nor is Jesus Christ. I would say, if we want to maintain the freedom our country has enjoyed so far, then we have to come to the realization that freedom without faith cannot survive.

We need to have a revival of faith to preserve our freedom. I pray that you will take your children to church and Sunday school or to a faith group every week.

At one of my book signings, a family—the husband and wife were nearing eighty—came to me and said, "We never had any religion, then we started watching you on the 'Hour of Power' thirty years ago." And with tears in their eyes, they said, "We have only one regret in our life, and it is that we never took our kids to church or Sunday school."

Freedom can be retained, attained, and then restrained appropriately, but it requires a Lord over your conscience. Then you shall know the truth, and the truth shall make you free.

~ROBERT SCHULLER I

What is a conscience?
IT IS REALLY THE PROOF OF GOD AND
THE MORAL LAW WITHIN.

~ ROBERT SCHULLER I

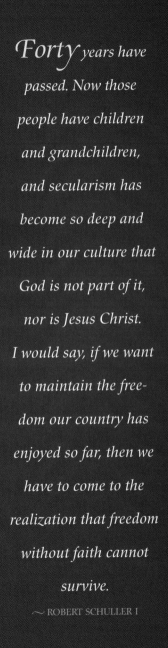

Forty years have passed. Now those people have children and grandchildren, and secularism has become so deep and wide in our culture that God is not part of it, nor is Jesus Christ. I would say, if we want to maintain the freedom our country has enjoyed so far, then we have to come to the realization that freedom without faith cannot survive.

~ ROBERT SCHULLER I

GODLY AFFIRMATIONS

ONE OF MY FAVORITE DAYS OF THE WEEK IS WEDNESDAY—
NOT ONLY BECAUSE FRIDAY IS JUST AROUND THE CORNER BUT
ALSO BECAUSE IT'S THE DAY I ATTEND AN INCREDIBLE BIBLE
STUDY WITH SOME VERY INSPIRING AND LOVING WOMEN IN
MY CHURCH. THE WISDOM AND INSIGHT THAT I GAIN FROM
THIS WEEKLY GATHERING IS SO PRICELESS THAT I PRAY THAT
EVERY WOMAN MIGHT BELONG TO SUCH A GROUP.

We recently finished a book entitled *Leaving a Godly
Legacy*, by Charles Stanley. My particular week for leading the
study fell on chapter six, which focused on the importance of
setting an example for children, specifically when relating to
other people. If our children see us treating others in a fair,
friendly, graceful, and loving way, then they most likely will
learn to treat others in the same way.

One of my favorite things to pass on to others is the

DO NOT LET ANY
UNWHOLESOME TALK
COME OUT OF YOUR
MOUTHS, BUT ONLY
WHAT IS HELPFUL FOR
BUILDING OTHERS UP
ACCORDING TO THEIR
NEEDS, THAT IT MAY
BENEFIT THOSE WHO
LISTEN.

EPHESIANS 4:29, NIV

importance of choosing encouraging words when relaying information to each other, especially to children. Parents—and any adult who has an opportunity to influence a child's life—should have a list of inspiring words. My list is posted in my pantry, a very visible place that I visit often. Even on days when I am not feeling like motivating or uplifting others, I can open this door and see this list staring me right in the eyes. Some of the words and phrases it contains are:

- Wow
- Way to Go
- Outstanding
- Excellent
- Great
- Good
- Neat
- Well Done
- Remarkable

- I'm Proud of You
- Fantastic
- Exceptional
- You're Doing Great
- You're a Joy
- I Respect You
- You've Got a Friend
- You Made My Day
- I Love You

This list is actually filled with at least one hundred more affirmations. I urge you to make a similar list of motivating and complimentary sayings. One very important way we can pass on a godly legacy of faith, hope, love, and success is to show others that we value them.

~ DONNA SCHULLER

ONE VERY IMPORTANT WAY WE CAN PASS
ON A GODLY LEGACY OF FAITH, HOPE, LOVE,
and success is to show others that we value them.

~ DONNA SCHULLER

Grandma's Pies

I recall a story that my father has often shared with me about my grandmother. My late Grandma Schuller lived in a small Iowa town where she made the finest pies in the world. I remember her as tall and big—but I especially remember her pies!

I remember gathering apples from her backyard. My sisters—Sheila and Jeanne—and I would peel them, and Grandma would dice them. Eventually, the pie was ready for the oven, and my grandmother would bake that pie just right until the crust would crack and the syrup would ooze out and run down the sides. She'd pull it out of the oven at just the right moment, and the aroma would fill the entire house. It was wonderful!

My father tells of how my grandmother would bake these pies and give them to people who were in need. One day, Grandma heard of a schoolteacher in town who was sick, and she baked her a pie. The schoolteacher thanked my grandmother for it, and that was the end of the story. . . or so we thought.

Fifteen years later, my father started televising the "Hour of Power" for the Crystal Cathedral. The schoolteacher heard about the church's need and looked in her checkbook, hoping to give a donation. She had never married and didn't have any children, and she realized that her checking account was full of money that she didn't need. So she wrote a check for twenty-two thousand dollars and sent it to the Crystal Cathedral.

In the letter that accompanied the check, she wrote: "Dear Dr. Schuller, Your mother once gave me an apple pie, and I know that apple pie wasn't worth twenty-two thousand dollars. Twenty maybe, but not twenty-two. I figure that since your mother was so good, there must be an awful lot of good in you too."

What happens when you perform random acts of kindness? A spark ignites in your heart. As you continue these acts, your heart and soul and mind begin to flow with the Living Waters that Jesus promised the woman at the well. The spark will infiltrate every area of your life, and you will begin to see life in a different, more positive way. ✒

~ ROBERT SCHULLER II

Be kindly affectionate to one another with brotherly love, in honor giving preference to one another; not lagging in diligence, fervent in spirit, serving the Lord.

ROMANS 12:10

What happens when you perform random acts of kindness?
A spark ignites in your heart.

~ ROBERT SCHULLER II

AN INVISIBLE SHIELD

GOD CAN AND WILL PROTECT YOU. HE HAS PROTECTED ME ALL MY LIFE FROM EVIL. HE PROTECTS US WITH AN INVISIBLE SHIELD OF FAITH, THE TEN COMMANDMENTS, SALVATION, AND SPIRITUAL DISCIPLINES LIKE PRAYER AND BIBLE READING. GOD DELIVERS US FROM EVIL WHEN WE BECOME A PART OF A COMMUNITY OF CARING PEOPLE IN A CHURCH OR A BIBLE STUDY GROUP.

Many years ago, shortly after World War II, my wife and I traveled to Berlin where I preached at the bombed-out Kaiser Wilhelm church in Berlin. In the congregation that day, an American woman became so emotional that she started crying. A German woman sitting on another side of the church saw her, got up from where she was sitting, crossed the aisle, and stood next to the American woman. She dried the American woman's tears and put her hand on her cheek. It was a perfect example of what a community of caring and supportive souls can do for one another.

Many religions believe in evil, but there's Someone out there who offers protection from evil: Jesus Christ. I invite

ABOVE ALL, TAKING THE SHIELD OF FAITH WITH WHICH YOU WILL BE ABLE TO QUENCH ALL THE FIERY DARTS OF THE WICKED ONE.

EPHESIANS 6:16

you to become a follower of Jesus Christ. Become a believer. It's a decision, not an argument, and because of your choice, God will deliver you from evil. Then find a group of people who practice spiritual disciplines and who will encourage you in your faith. ✒

~ ROBERT SCHULLER I

Let It Rain

I was fifteen and on a mission trip in Thailand when I witnessed my very first miracle. Until that point, a miracle had always been just a story in the Bible or a gimmick of a traveling evangelist, but when I witnessed this event, my view of the supernatural was changed forever.

My team and I were traveling to villages to share the Gospel of Christ. In one particular village, we stayed in a hut that was unbelievable, like something out of a book or movie. It was elevated about five feet in order to survive the many floods, and its roof was made of tin, palm branches, and bamboo. The people who lived there were

Rejoice always, pray without ceasing, in everything give thanks.
1 THESSALONIANS 5:16–17

believers, the kindest souls I had ever met, and they made a living by farming rice and chicken. Our team had spent an entire week in this little province, but we experienced little to no success.

As we were loading the trucks to travel to our last ministry site in the area, our hosts asked us to pray for their new church of twenty-eight people, and they asked us to pray for rain. We learned that there had been a drought in the area for three months, a very rare occurrence for the monsoon season. As a result, the people were suffering because they couldn't grow rice or feed their chickens. Suddenly, we understood the people's unwelcoming response to the Gospel.

As we prayed and interceded for these people, I could literally feel the presence of God. About two minutes after we said "amen," it began to sprinkle, and then it started to pour. I was astonished!

In the rain, we traveled to the school, which was our last stop. Before we reached the gates, however, the principal came running out; he was yelling and worshiping us for the rain. "No! No!" we cried. "We didn't bring the rain, but we brought a message about the One who brought the rain." We then led the whole school and faculty to Christ.

Jesus was victorious, and the rain continued for three days straight.

~ ROBERT SCHULLER III

Family First

A few years ago, a friend of mine was working on his Ph.D. while he was also working full-time in his job. His studies and work kept him away from home most of the time. One night, when he came home late, he saw a picture that his daughter had drawn in school. The title of the picture was "Our Family Best."

As my friend looked at the picture, he saw his two sons, his daughter, and his wife, but he wasn't included. His daughter had left him out. Suddenly, the reality of his actions hit hard. *What have I been doing?* he said to himself. *I'm not even in the family picture anymore. My daughter doesn't even know I'm her daddy.*

The next day, he went to his wife and said, "Honey, I want to come home." And he came home and became a daddy once again to his little girl and his sons. A couple of years later, his daughter drew another picture of the family. This time, she drew her brothers and her mommy, and holding her hand was her daddy.

> *The Spirit Himself bears witness with our spirit that we are children of God, and if children, then heirs—heirs of God and joint heirs of Christ.*
>
> **ROMANS 8:16–17**

Time spent with your family is the most precious gift you can give. If you've been too busy for your loved ones, remember that you can always come home. You are an important part of your family—on earth and in the body of Christ.

~ ROBERT SCHULLER II

Time spent with your family
is the most precious gift you can give.

~ ROBERT SCHULLER II

Section
III

Mature... Hope

LIVE YOUR PURPOSE

ONE OF THE GREAT INFLUENCES OF MY LIFE WAS DR.
VIKTOR FRANKL. IN MY MIND, DR. FRANKL WAS PROBABLY
THE PREMIER PSYCHIATRIST OF THE TWENTIETH CENTURY.
HE DIED RECENTLY AT THE AGE OF NINETY-TWO.
I'VE LEARNED SO MUCH FROM HIS BOOKS, HIS LECTURES,
AND HIS FRIENDSHIP, BUT HE MADE ONE STATEMENT IN
PARTICULAR THAT I'LL NEVER FORGET: "THE 'IS' MUST
NEVER CATCH UP WITH THE 'OUGHT.'"

Dr. Frankl taught me that a purpose must be continually
within our lives to impassion us. If our goals have been
realized, then we need a new goal.

In the Old Testament, God guided the Israelites to the
Promised Land. How? By a pillar of fire at night and a pillar of cloud during the day. God stayed with His people,
urging them forward by His amazing presence.

A quarter of a century ago, I developed a theological
framework based on positive self-esteem. I preach it every
week to an audience that is of a size I cannot number. At
the basis of that framework is feeling proud of who you
are. I've never gone to bed ashamed of what I did or who

I was, though probably every night, I have had to ask for-giveness from God for my sins. But sins are no excuse for inflicting shame on your soul. When you know the Friend that I have, and His name is Jesus Christ, then you know that He loves you even though you're not perfect. With Jesus as your Friend, you can believe in yourself, and you will have a purpose to impassion you.

For what or whom are you living? I don't live for kicks. I don't look for stimulation that will excite me. Instead, I seek a purpose that will give me a reason for living.

What is my purpose? It's a person. His name is Jesus Christ. ✍

~ ROBERT SCHULLER I

FOR TO ME, TO LIVE IS CHRIST, AND TO DIE IS GAIN.

PHILIPPIANS 1:21

What is my purpose?
IT'S A PERSON.
HIS NAME IS JESUS CHRIST.

~ ROBERT SCHULLER I

Giving to God

Allow me to ask you a question: Does everything you have belong to God?

I love the mission field, but my travels are not free. I love to go to a nation that is dark and tormented by sin and show the people the goodness of the blood of Jesus. I love to show them how special they are and how much He loves them. But I'm just a young man without a job, so how can I afford to take this message to people who need to hear it? The church pays for these trips, the members of the body of Christ, and I've done some pretty crazy things to get people to give.

I remember when my friend Dave Victorine and I went door-to-door saying, "I'll sell you this egg for a dollar, or I'll break it over my head for three." This practice became quite rewarding as we earned over three hundred dollars and got really shiny hair. That money, though, helped me reach Russian Gypsies and that money gave new hope to old Russian men.

I feel joy in being obedient to God, and I have experienced the reward of His blessings. God will also bless your giving; your tithes can reach lost and dying people.

Now let me ask the question again: Does everything you have belong to God? If so, then giving is only transferring money from one of God's accounts to another.

~ ROBERT SCHULLER III

So let each one give as he purposes in his heart, not grudgingly or of necessity; for God loves a cheerful giver.

2 CORINTHIANS 9:7

I FEEL JOY IN BEING OBEDIENT TO GOD,
and I have experienced the reward of His blessings.

~ ROBERT SCHULLER III

Who Owns You?

I like used furniture, and we have a lot of used furniture in our house. I recently purchased a fabulous desk at a moving sale, probably one of the finest desks money can buy. It is made by Sly Furniture, a corporation in Holland, Michigan, who is known as a maker of great desks. I'd been looking for one like it for a long time, but I just hadn't been able to afford it. But there it was, on sale for $150. If I were going to buy a brand-new desk like it, then I probably would have to pay $1,000 or more.

There are some circumstances, though, when used furniture goes for a high price. Consider the amount of money collected from Jackie Onassis' estate sale. Among the many items for sale was a very fine used desk, which was appraised at $100,000 before the auctions. I was shocked when it actually sold for over a million dollars!

What's the difference? What makes her desk so much more valuable than mine? Only one thing: it belonged to Jackie Onassis! Her desk was significant because she owned it, and whatever she owned was worth a lot of money.

Here's a question for you: Where do you find your worth in life? Who owns you? When you own yourself, you place a price on your worth, but when God owns you, you are invaluable! Priceless beyond compare! Words can't express the potential and the value in you. When you're owned by God, when you're called by Him and following His ways and His will, then you are significant. ✒

~ ROBERT SCHULLER II

I have called you by your name; You are Mine.

ISAIAH 43:1

When you own yourself, you place a price on your worth, but when God owns you, you are invaluable! Priceless beyond compare!

~ ROBERT SCHULLER II

A LEGACY REMEMBERED

ALTHOUGH I NEVER HAD THE CHANCE TO MEET HIM,
I HAVE OFTEN HEARD A STORY TOLD OF ANTHONY
SCHULLER. HE WAS MY FATHER-IN-LAW'S FATHER AND
MY HUSBAND'S GRANDFATHER. OUR YOUNGEST SON,
ANTHONY, ALSO CARRIES ON HIS NAME—AND HIS SPIRIT
OF PERSEVERANCE.

Grandpa Anthony left the greatest gift a man can leave
to a family; he left a legacy of success. Few have recognized
that legacy, however, because he never received any significant awards, he wasn't a community leader, and he didn't
leave a large inheritance. Instead, the legacy he left was a
faith in God that translates into a positive mental attitude
and an indomitable spirit that never quits. With these two
qualities, anyone can become a champion.

My father-in-law, Robert I, was fortunate to be the only
one out of five children in his family to receive a four-year
college education. One summer, when he was nineteen
years old, he came home from his studies at Hope College
in Holland, Michigan. One particular day, the family sat
outside of their little farmhouse, watching the sky. The
weather was extremely turbulent, and they could tell that

BLESSED ARE THOSE WHO PUT THEIR TRUST IN HIM.

PSALM 2:12

something terrible was about to happen. And it did. Off in the distance, they watched the funnel appear. It snaked its way down to the ground and started making its way straight toward them! They ran to their car to escape, but because they lived on a dead-end road, they had to drive directly toward the tornado to get away from it.

They edged down the side of the road until they could turn down a side street. Then from a safe distance, they waited and watched until the horrific twister was sucked back into the sky, somberly and silently. As they drove back to the farm, they looked for the landmarks that told them they were almost home, but they couldn't see anything familiar—no trees sticking above the crest of the hill, no barn or shed to herald their homecoming. Everything was gone! The foundations were all that remained. They found the house a quarter of a mile away, smashed into pieces.

The family discovered that they were not the only ones to lose everything. There were four other families who also were homeless and financially destitute. But Anthony told his family to be thankful to God for being alive. He said, "Never look at what you've lost; always look at what you have left." Then with the meager insurance money that he received, Anthony Schuller did what no one else was able to do. At the age of seventy, he was the only one of the five families to rebuild.

With the little they had, the family started over again, and within a few years, they built a modest little farm with a house and a collection of other buildings. Anthony was able to retire securely as his oldest son, Henry, continued to work the farm. Eventually, Henry bought the farm and lived there until he retired only a few years ago.

You may not have fortune, gold medals, or a famous name to pass on to your children, but you can give them hope! You can give them a faith in God that builds the character of legacies. That is success! I have seen this hope through faith passed on from one generation to the next in the Schuller family. You can give the same kind of hope and faith to your children. Live it, and watch it grow. ✍

~ DONNA SCHULLER

You may not have fortune, gold medals, or a famous name to pass on to your children, but you can give them hope! You can give them a faith in God that builds the character of legacies.

~ DONNA SCHULLER

THE POWER OF COMMITMENT

WHY DOES COMMITMENT RELEASE SUCH INCREDIBLE, IMMENSE DIVINE ENERGY AND POWER?

When you set a goal and make a commitment, you feel alive, but if you hesitate and play the field of ambiguity, then you'll pay an enormous price. You'll lose energy, enthusiasm, dynamism, and vitality.

COMMIT YOUR WAY TO THE LORD, AND HE SHALL GIVE YOU THE DESIRES OF YOUR HEART.

PSALM 37:5

When you make a commitment:

- A decision is made.
- Enthusiasm is released.
- Apathy disappears.
- Excellence is targeted.
- Leadership is asserted.
- Faith takes control of your future.
- You're free to grow.
- You receive optimism and hope.
- You become a spiritual creature.
- You are affirmed as a person.
- Success is honored.
- A direction is established.
- Fears are overpowered.
- Your life is focused.
- Opportunities can become achievements.
- Youth is renewed.
- Relationships are expanded.
- Your power base is extended.
- Your priorities are established.
- Your vision is crystallized.

I sincerely encourage you to make a commitment to the Bible. It has been around for over three thousand years, and it will never die out because its words are the Truth. I encourage you to make a commitment to the Jesus Christ of the Bible. Study Him. Listen to Him. It's a commitment you will never regret.

— ROBERT SCHULLER I

You become a
spiritual creature A Apat

LEADERSHIP IS Enthusi
ASSERTED Opportunities can
become achievemen

A decision is O V
You are a
made
A direction is established

YOU RECEIVE
AND HOPE Re
Fears are overpowered

Success is honored Exce
You

STUDY HIM.

Listen to Him.

IT'S A COMMITMENT YOU WILL NEVER REGRET.

~ ROBERT SCHULLER I

The Joy of the Lord

I will never forget a story my dad told me about joy.

There were two twin boys, one who had a very positive outlook on life and one who had a very negative outlook on life. In light of this, some scientists came together to see how these boys would react in certain environments. First, they took the boy with the negative outlook and put him in a room full of all sorts of games and toys. Then they took the boy with the positive outlook and put him in a room full of horse manure. They left the boys for one hour and came back for the results.

In the first room, they found the boy with the negative outlook crying, even though he was surrounded by toys and games. The scientists asked, "What's the matter?" The boy answered, "I have so many toys that I don't know which one to play with first." Shaking their heads and sighing, they moved on to the next room full of manure. To their surprise, they saw the little boy covered in manure, leaping up and down, laughing, and throwing manure all around the room. They stopped him and with great amazement asked, "Why are you so happy?" The boy replied, "With all this pony poop around, there's got to be a pony in here somewhere!"

Joy is being excited about life, regardless of what situa-

Do not sorrow,
for the joy of
the Lord is
your strength.

NEHEMIAH 8:10

tion you're in. I love this story because it shows how one's attitude can change his or her environment.

Christ's sacrifice gives us a supernatural joy that changes our circumstances and the lives of the people around us. So live! Suck the marrow out of the life that God has given you and experience *His* joy. 🌿

~ ROBERT SCHULLER III

CHRIST'S SACRIFICE GIVES US A
SUPERNATURAL JOY THAT CHANGES OUR
CIRCUMSTANCES AND THE LIVES OF THE
PEOPLE AROUND US.

~ ROBERT SCHULLER III

Staying the Course

I enjoy sportfishing in the ocean. It's my hobby. I usually leave early in the morning while it's still dark. My fishing partners and I motor about fifty miles offshore, zigzagging in every direction. We sometimes follow birds and porpoise, looking for just the right fishing conditions. Eventually, however, we have no concept of where we are.

At the end of the day, when it's time to go home, we look around, and guess what we see? Everywhere we look, we see exactly the same thing: water. Lots and lots of water, in every direction. And it all looks the same. It's all blue, and it's all wet. Until we figure out where in the world we are, we have absolutely no idea which way to go, or which way is home.

Fortunately, we take along a device called a Global Position System (GPS). It is sold in most sporting goods stores. Many boaters, fishermen, hunters, and campers use this instrument to find out where they are while at sea, in the mountains, or in the wilderness. At any place in the world, the GPS can give the latitude and longitude of your position.

And whatever things you ask in prayer, believing, you will receive.

MATTHEW 2:22

After my fishing partners and I find our coordinates, we draw a line from where we are to the homeport. Then, we steer a course that will take us right into the harbor. After we travel about twenty-five miles, we check our course again. Sometimes, it is off about five degrees because of winds, waves, and currents, so we reposition. Pretty soon, we see the port, and we are home. Isn't it wonderful? I never get lost, as long as the GPS works.

Prayer is our GPS to God. When we pray, we can ask, "God, where am I? Who am I? Where do you want me to go? What course corrections do I need to take in my life? Get me back on the path, Lord." That's what prayer is . . . connecting to God. It's your guide to home.

~ ROBERT SCHULLER II

That's what prayer is...

Connecting to God

IT'S YOUR GUIDE TO HOME.

~ ROBERT SCHULLER II

THE LEGACY

LAST YEAR, MY WIFE, ARVELLA, AND I WENT TO HAWAII TO CELEBRATE OUR FORTY-NINTH WEDDING ANNIVERSARY. WE USED THIS TIME TO REFLECT ON THE INCREDIBLE LEGACY THAT OUR FAMILIES LEFT TO US AND WHAT WE, IN TURN, HAVE PASSED ON TO OUR CHILDREN.

We were both born to simple Iowa farm families and devout Dutch people. We grew up going to church every Sunday and read the Bible in our homes every day. We prayed every morning, noon, and night. As children, we went to Sunday school every single Sunday without exception.

My testimony is that God can do great things through a family that loves Him. God has blessed my father and mother and and their family, my wife and her family, and the family my wife and I had together.

For our forty-ninth wedding anniversary, we stopped the clock and took a long look at what has happened to us since we recited our marriage vows. God didn't promise us that we would live more than a year—or five or ten. He didn't prom-ise us that we would have ten, twenty, thirty, or forty—to say nothing of forty-nine, almost fifty years—together! He didn't promise us that we would have children, and we had five. I am truly very proud of each of my children.

All of my children love the Lord and love the church, and all are in some form of ministry. Each of my children married a Christian spouse. They all read the Bible in their homes every day, and they pray in their homes every day. They also attend church every Sunday, and their children go to Sunday school every week. Their families all love the Lord in their Christian homes. And they have given my wife and I eighteen grandchildren, whom we adore!

We never knew that on our forty-ninth wedding anniversary we would get a beautiful orchid plant from all of our five children. The card that came with it said, "Dear Mom and Dad, Thank you for showing us what love looks like." 🌿

~ ROBERT SCHULLER I

IN EVERYTHING SET THEM AN EXAMPLE BY DOING WHAT IS GOOD.

TITUS 2:7, NIV

GOD HAS BLESSED MY FATHER AND MOTHER
and their family, my wife and her family,
and the family my wife and I had together.

~ ROBERT SCHULLER I

My Family's Legacy of Success